Word Study

Improving Usage and Meaning
Book 2
Grades 4-5

Written by Jenny Nitert and Debra Salerno
Published by World Teachers Press®

Published with the permission of R.I.C. Publications Pty. Ltd.

First published by R.I.C. Publications Pty. Ltd., Perth, Western Australia.

Printed in the United States of America.

Order Number 2-5141
ISBN 1-58324-065-9

A B C D E F 03 02 01 00 99

Educational Resources
395 Main Street
Rowley, MA 01969
www.worldteacherspress.com

Word Study: Improving Usage and Meaning

Introduction

Word Study: Improving Usage and Meaning is a series of four blackline master books for grades two to eight. Each book provides 42 pages of interesting activities promoting vocabulary development, comprehension and usage.

An answer key is provided at the back of each book for your convenience in correcting the student activity pages.

The series includes:

Word Study: Improving Usage and Meaning	**Grades 2-3**
Word Study: Improving Usage and Meaning	**Grades 4-5**
Word Study: Improving Usage and Meaning	**Grades 6-7**
Word Study: Improving Usage and Meaning	**Grades 7-8**

Contents

Teachers Notes

Introduction:

Word Study plays an important role in the development of students' understanding of the English language. They develop a knowledge of how words work and why certain words are used in the manner they are. This book is designed to take students through a range of word study topics which aim to develop understanding, word knowledge, usage and a larger range of words the students can use with confidence in their day-to-day experiences.

Suggested Lesson Development:

The activities within this book are grouped according to topics. Topics can be used in any order depending upon the requirements of the students in your classroom. Each topic develops sequentially and should be used in order to ensure development from the simplest concept to the most difficult concept occurs.

Step 1: Select a topic. For example, antonyms. Photocopy enough worksheets for each child.

Step 2: Carry out discussion about antonyms before handing out the worksheet. Establish the class's understanding or preconceived ideas of what an antonym is. If students are familiar with antonyms, brainstorm some examples to begin the lesson.

Step 3: Distribute copies of the worksheets to each student. Discuss the expectations and instructions of the worksheet. Point out to the students the definition of an antonym. Review their definition and compare. Read through the worksheet and point out any words the students may have difficulty with.

Step 4: Students complete the worksheet to the best of their ability. Answer any questions the children may have in relation to the worksheet.

Step 5: Collect the completed worksheets. Discuss antonyms and ask for students to give examples. This will establish the class's understanding of the topic. Marking of the worksheets should focus on the accuracy of students' answers not their spelling of the words.

Extension: Students can work toward making a class Antonym Dictionary as reference material to be used by all the students in the class.

Students can complete further activities within this topic and other topics within this book to extend knowledge.

Glossary of Terms used in this Book:

Abbreviation: A word which is made shorter by leaving out some letters. For example, Dr. – Doctor.

Adjective: A word which describes a noun. They give the reader more information. For example, the big, brown dog ate the fat, juicy steak quickly.

Adverb: A word which adds descriptions to verbs. These tell the reader how, where and when it is done. For example, walk slowly or run quickly.

Anagram: A word formed by rearranging the letters in another word. For example, ate becomes tea or eat.

Antonym: A word which has an opposite meaning to another word. For example, fast and slow.

Collective Noun: A word that names a collection of animals or things. For example, a school of fish.

Compound Word: A word made by joining two separate words together. For example, fire + place = fireplace.

Contraction: Words which are made shorter by taking out letters and adding an apostrophe. For example, is + not = isn't.

Homograph: Words which are spelled the same but have a different meaning. For example, nails – finger nails and nails used in wood.

Homophone: Words which have the same sound but a different spelling. For example, sea and see.

Plural: When making some words plural (more than one), you only need to add and 's,' For example, ball – balls.

Words that end in 'ss,' 'x,' 'sh,' 'ch' and 'o,' add an 'es' when there is more than one. Other words only need 's' to make them more than one.

When some words end in 'y' change the 'y' to 'i' and add 'es' to make them plural. For example, puppy – puppies.

Prefix: A word part which is added to the front of a word to change the meaning.

Suffix: A word part added to the end of a word to change the meaning.

Synonym: A word which has nearly the same meaning to another word. For example, little and small.

Verb: A word which states an action. For example, run, walk, hop, jump, cook, etc.

PREFIXES - 1

1. Find six words for each *prefix* in the word search and list them below.

E			H	T	U	O	C	N	U	P	D			D
V			S	R	A	L	U	C	O	N	I	B		I
O	E	U	N	A	B	L	E	V	M	R	A	S	I	D	S
R	P	N	O	E	E	N	L	A	U	N	N	A	I	B	E	U	A
P	N	E	S	L	V	P	D	I	S	A	P	P	E	A	R	N	G
P	S	V	A	C	U	N	K	N	O	W	N	P			C	R
A	N	E	I	Y	N	B	I	S	E	C	T	O			O	E
S	V	N	P	C	Q	T	U	N	A	L	E	I			V	E
I	N	I	K	I	B	R	S	D	I	A	P	N	U		E	N
D	I	S	A	B	L	E	B	I	C	E	N	T	E	N	A	R	Y

dis_____   bi_____   un_____

dis_____   bi_____   un_____

dis_____   bi_____   un_____

dis_____   bi_____   un_____

dis_____   bi_____   un_____

dis_____   bi_____   un_____

2. Write the first two words in each list in separate sentences on the back of this page. The sentence must show the meaning of each word.

1. Find what these *prefixes* mean. Write an example.

Prefix	Meaning	Example
re		
sub		
mis		

2. Write five words that use these *prefixes*.

re_____	sub_____	mis_____
re_____	sub_____	mis_____
re_____	sub_____	mis_____
re_____	sub_____	mis_____
re_____	sub_____	mis_____

3. Match each *prefix* to its meaning.

anti	•	•	three
bi	•	•	before
auto	•	•	not
dis	•	•	two
post	•	•	against
pre	•	•	self
tri	•	•	apart from, not
un	•	•	after

4. Choose two words on this page. Write each one in a sentence that shows the meaning of the word.

(a) _____

_____

(b) _____

_____

The **prefix** 're' means 'to do again.'
For example, heat - **re**heat.

1. Add the *prefix* 're' to each word below only if it makes a new word. Use a dictionary to help you.

_____pay   _____paint   _____write

_____happy   _____do   _____sleep

_____arrange   _____print   _____wind

2. Choose three *'re'* words and write each of them in an interesting sentence.

1. _____

    _____

2. _____

    _____

3. _____

    _____

3. Answer true or false. Circle the *'under'* words.

The **prefix** 'under' means under or beneath.

A fish lives underground. _____

The opposite of overarm is underarm. _____

A bird can fly underwater. _____

An elephant wears underwear. _____

The **prefix** 'bi' means two.
The **prefix** 'tri' means three.

bicycle

binoculars

4. Draw these *'tri'* and *'bi'* words.

tricycle

Suffixes - 1

> **Suffix** *a word part which is put at the end of a word to change the meaning.*
> *For example, ful: meaning 'full of' - powerful.*

1. Here are some meanings of words.
    Write each word and use it in a sentence.

(a) Full of pain

(b) Full of beauty

(c) Full of fright

(d) Full of uses

(e) Full of taste

(a) _____

_____

(b) _____

_____

(c) _____

_____

(d) _____

_____

(e) _____

_____

2. Think of nine more words that use a *suffix* to make words mean 'full of.'

_____ _____ _____

_____ _____ _____

_____ _____ _____

'ese' is a suffix that indicates a person from a particular country.

Suffixes - 2

'ist' is a suffix that often indicates an occupation. For example, one who works in biology is a biologist.

'hood' is a suffix that means 'the state of being.' For example, brotherhood.

1. Choose the correct *suffix* to add to the words below. Write the meaning of the new words you have made.

Word	Word with suffix	Meaning
Taiwan		
chemistry		
geology		
Japan		
parent		
father		
violin		
mother		
China		
guitar		

2. Write two more words that use the *suffix*:

(a) hood _____

_____

(b) ist _____

_____

(c) ese _____

_____

The **suffix** 'less' means 'without.'
For example, fearless - without fear.

SUFFIXES - 3

1. The words in the crossword puzzle have the *suffix* 'less.' Use the clues to fill in the missing words.

Across

2. Without use
6. Without care
8. Without end
9. Without hope
10. Without rest

Down

1. Without fear
3. Without help
4. Without taste
5. Without a home
7. Without sense

2. Choose a 'less' word from the crossword puzzle above to complete the sentences.

(a) The gravy for the meat was _____ .

(b) If you are _____ an accident can happen.

(c) The long drive through the country seemed _____ .

(d) Many people were left _____ after their houses were damaged in the storm.

Suffixes - 4

The **suffix** 'ful' means 'full of'. For example, help - helpful.

1. Add 'ful' to these words and write the new word in the sentence.

Word	Sentence
teaspoon	The boy had a _____ of sugar in his tea.
mouth	The girl had a _____ of cake and could not talk.
pain	The child's broken arm was very _____.
cup	The cook used a _____ of flour in the cake.

2. Answer yes or no. Circle the 'ful' words.

(a) Do you feel cheerful?   _____

(b) Is a rainbow colorful?   _____

(c) Is a flower garden beautiful?   _____

(d) Is the sun harmful to our skin? _____

The **suffix** 'er' can mean 'one who'. a teacher is one who teaches.

3. Unjumble these 'er' words.

rfmera

rgaerdne

_____

tripane

kebra

_____

Antonyms - 1

1. Find the *antonyms* (opposites) to these words in the word search.

   (a) nobody _____

   (b) rise _____

   (c) forget _____

   (d) absent _____

   (e) midnight _____

   (f) fresh _____

   (g) enemy _____

   (h) together _____

   (i) arrive _____

   (j) import _____

   (k) useful _____

   (l) brave _____

   (m) obey _____

   (n) rough _____

   (o) entrance _____

D	T	R	A	P	E	D	H
Y	I	D	O	U	G	T	D
B	O	N	V	R	U	S	I
P	R	E	S	E	N	T	S
S	S	I	H	M	R	A	O
E	S	R	P	E	B	L	B
A	E	F	V	M	N	E	E
L	L	O	A	B	F	L	Y
E	E	G	D	E	X	I	T
V	S	N	T	R	A	P	A
E	U	Y	E	H	B	Y	C
R	D	H	X	T	N	L	I
Y	R	U	P	O	A	D	W
B	V	E	O	O	C	R	D
O	J	T	R	M	S	A	K
D	F	O	T	S	P	W	B
Y	A	D	D	I	M	O	Q
G	L	F	A	L	L	C	M

2. Use a dictionary to find *antonyms* for these.

   (a) regular _____   (b) sincere _____

   (c) seldom _____   (d) respect _____

Antonyms - 2

1. Unjumble the words. Match the word to its *antonym*.

	Word	Antonym
rrofwad	forward	alive
tiWner		guilty
deda		correct
epon		backward
nmcnuomo		shut
olcse		open
olw		Summer
ncninoet		happy
yanuhpp		common
crocinret		high

2. Change these words, one letter at a time, to their *antonyms*. Each time you change a letter, a new word must be formed. For example,

WARM
w(o)r m
w o r(d)
w o(o)d
w o o(l)
COOL

WILD

TAME

FALL

HATE

LOVE

RISE

B	O	T	T	O	M	Y	O	B	D	R	Y
E	S	W	H	G	U	A	L	P	E	S	O
L	N	O	C	N	I	G	H	T	E	M	U
O	H	L	W	O	L	S	W	F	P	A	N
W	C	W	O	R	R	A	N	D	K	L	G
F	I	R	S	T	B	M	W	O	J	L	T
F	R	D	W	S	D	L	O	C	T	R	U
O	U	T	S	I	D	E	D	R	E	V	O

1.
Find the *antonym* for each word in the word search.

last _____

poor _____

old _____

girl _____

hot _____

weak _____

wet _____

up _____

on _____

in _____

top _____

shallow _____

day _____

large _____

inside _____

fast _____

under _____

wide _____

above _____

cry _____

high _____

2. Read the sentence. Change the bold words to *antonyms*.
The **old lady frowned** at the puppy.

_____

_____

Draw a picture of the sentence.

Synonyms - 1

1. Find *synonyms* for these words to complete the crossword puzzle.

Across

4. beautiful
6. mistake
7. choose
8. angry
9. happy
10. voyage
12. engine
13. tame
14. finish

Down

1. simple
2. wind
3. strange
5. timber
8. lots
9. start
11. zero

2. Find *synonyms* for:
(a) deadly

_____

_____

(b) cease

_____

_____

(c) placid

_____

_____

Synonyms - 2

1. Find three *synonyms* for each word.

big

rock

knock

yell

stream

boat

break

throw

look

2. List two ways *synonyms* can help us improve our writing.

(a) _____

(b) _____

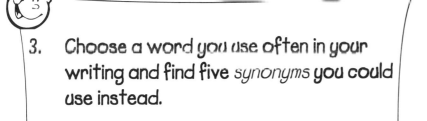

3. Choose a word you use often in your writing and find five *synonyms* you could use instead.

_____ _____

_____ _____

_____

1. **Write each sentence.**
   Change the *bold* **words to** *synonyms.*

(a) The **boat** steamed out of port.

   _____

(b) The castle was **enormous.**

   _____

(c) Are you **afraid** of the dark?

   _____

(d) I like to keep my desk **tidy.**

   _____

2. **Draw a circle around the** *synonyms.*

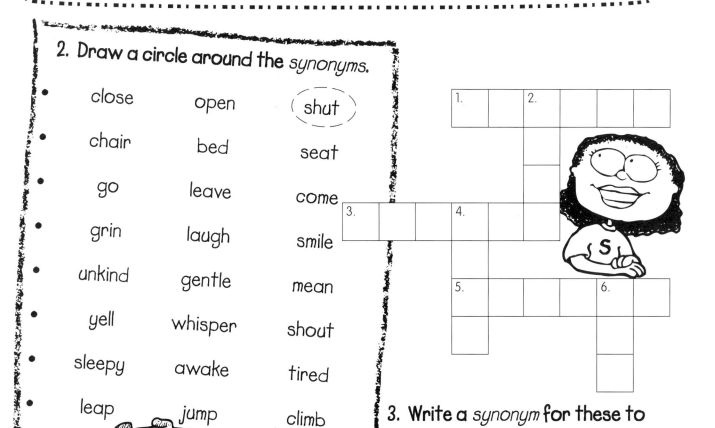

- close   open   (shut)
- chair   bed   seat
- go   leave   come
- grin   laugh   smile
- unkind   gentle   mean
- yell   whisper   shout
- sleepy   awake   tired
- leap   jump   climb

1.		2.		

|3. | | |4. | | |

|5. | | |6. | |

3. **Write a** *synonym* **for these to**
   complete the crossword puzzle.

(1) beautiful   (2) simple
(3) thin   (4) close
(5) nearly   (6) ocean

Homophones	Are words that sound the same but are spelled differently. For example, knows and nose.

Homophones

1. Find *homophones* **for these words.**

    (a) flower   _____

    (b) four   _____

    (c) boar   _____

    (d) sale   _____

2. **Circle the correct** *homophone* **to complete these sentences.**

    (a) Did you (sea/see) that dog's long (tail/ tale)?

    (b) The (whole/hole) family went to the (fare/fair) over the school holidays.

    (c) The wind (blue/blew) and the (rain/reign) fell all (threw/through) the night.

3. **Match the** *homophones* **to their correct meanings.**

    (a) cue   •   •   a single line of people cars, animals, etc. waiting in turn for something.

    (b) queue   •   •   a small specially-shaped piece of metal that can open a lock.

    (c) quay   •   •   a long stick used to hit a ball in billiards.

    (d) key   •   •   a wharf where ships and ferries load or unload passengers or cargo.

List 10 homophone pairs on the back of this page.

Homophones and Homographs

1. **Complete the crossword puzzle below by using** *homophones* **to the clues.**

Across

2. wear
5. here
6. which
8. pair
10. I
11. steal
12. cheep
15. eight
16. right

Down

1. war
2. way
3. bail
4. their
7. sent
8. pole
9. knew
11. see
13. plane
14. mail

> Words which are spelled the same but have different meanings are called **homographs**.
>
> For example, nails — fingernails and nails used in wood.

2. **Show the meanings of these** *homographs.*

bill

bill

3. Find three more *homographs.*

_____

_____

_____

1. The pictures below show the different meanings for the *homograph* 'bat.' Write a sentence for each.

_____

_____

_____

2. Draw pictures to show the different meanings for these *homographs*.

| rock | rock | | fly | fly |

3. Unjumble the *homographs*. Write sentences to show the different meanings.

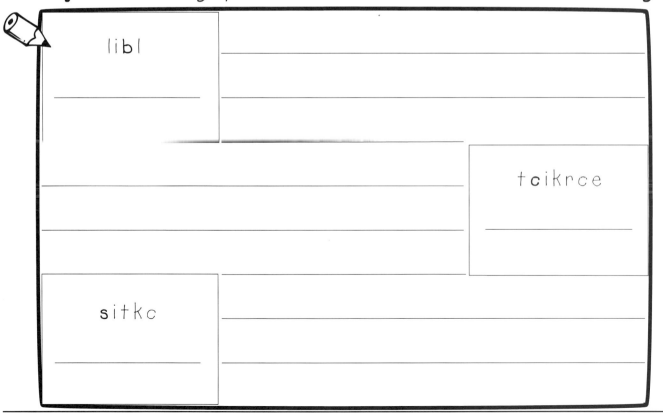

libl

_____

tcikrce

_____

sitkc

_____

1. Write *contractions* **for these words.**

   (a) they will _____

   (b) have not _____

   (c) there is _____

   (d) we are _____

   (e) you have _____

   (f) I am _____

   (g) let us _____

   (h) I would _____

---

2. **Use these** *contractions* **to complete the sentences.**

   I'll   hasn't   shouldn't   should've   haven't

   (a) I _____ seen my cat for days. I hope she

   _____ run away.

   (b) My brother _____ ride his bicycle without his helmet.

   Mom is going to be angry with him.

   (c) I _____ cleaned up my room at the weekend. Now

   _____ probably miss out on my allowance.

3. **Unjumble these** *contractions* **and place the apostrophe.**

   (a) sthat _____

   (b) vclodue _____

   (c) htyde _____

   (d) hrewes _____

Contractions - 2

1. Match each of these words to its *contraction*.

do not •	• we've
that is •	• isn't
it is •	• don't
is not •	• what's
we have •	• didn't
they have •	• they've
did not •	• she's
you have •	• I've
she is •	• you've
what is •	• weren't
were not •	• I've
I have •	• it's
	• that's

2. Write *contractions* for these.

let us

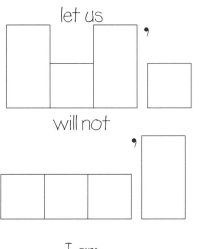

will not

I am

3. Sort the *contractions* above into family groups. Add one more to each group.

've	't	's

4. Choose a *contraction* from those above to complete each sentence.

(a) _____ the time please?

(b) _____ waiting for me.

(c) When _____ eaten your lunch, you may go play.

(d) They _____ allowed to go to the movies.

1. Write the *plural* for these.

man ☐☐☐

child ☐☐☐☐☐

foot ☐☐☐☐

woman ☐☐☐☐☐

*Some words change when making them **plural**. For example, tooth – teeth.*

> Words that end in 'ss,' 'x,' 'sh,' 'ch' and 'o' add an 'es' to make **plural.**

2. Write the *plural* of these words.

(a) echo _____

(b) bunch _____

(c) dress _____

(d) potato _____

(e) box _____

(f) glass _____

(g) brush _____

(h) lunch _____

*Words that end in 'y' can be made into **plurals** in two ways:*
- *change the 'y' to 'i' and add 'es;' for example, berry – berries.*
- *when the 'y' has a vowel before it, add an 's;' for example, donkey – donkeys.*

*Some words do not change at all for the **plural.** For example, deer, scissors and sheep.*

3. Write the *plural* of these to complete the crossword puzzle.

6. fly   1. chimney
3. lolly   4. enemy
2. holiday   5. daisy

plurals - 2

| Many words that end with 'f' or 'fe' change to 'v' before adding 'es' to make **plural**. For example, half - halves. |

1. **Write the correct word in the space.**

(a) The _____ (knife, knives) was very sharp.

(b) The farmer herded all the _____ (calf, calves) into the paddock.

(c) In autumn the _____ (leaf, leaves) fall from the trees.

(d) The freshly baked _____ (loaf, loaves) of bread was delicious.

2. **Write the *plural* of each word and find it in the word search.**

```
B U T T E R F L I E S X F
E W S Y E K N O M S Y F L
N I H S D S E O G R A C I
C S E O T A M O T E D S V
H H L W O L V E S G K E E
E E V S H E E P E N E X S
S S E S S I K H T I Y O L
T R S S E I R I A F S F M
```

finger   _____   life   _____

shelf   _____   day   _____

tomato   _____   monkey   _____

bench   _____   butterfly   _____

key   _____   fox   _____

fairy   _____   wolf   _____

wish   _____   cargo   _____

kiss   _____   sheep   _____

Words are often borrowed from other languages. The root word 'finis' is taken from the Latin language and means 'the end.' In English, this root word is used to make words such as final, finish and finite.

Word Origins

1. Sort these word parts into their origin groups. Find their meanings hidden in the word search.

   phon, circum, forma, derm, astro, bene, scribe, geo, photo, aqua

	Word	Meaning
GREEK		
GREEK		
GREEK		
GREEK		
GREEK		
LATIN		
LATIN		
LATIN		
LATIN		
LATIN		

S	O	U	N	D	B
H	R	E	O	L	Q
A	D	T	R	I	D
P	W	I	A	G	N
E	A	R	T	H	U
L	T	W	S	T	O
L	E	M	G	E	R
E	R	I	N	G	A
W	U	N	I	K	S

2. Choose one Greek and one Latin root from above. List words that use the root you have chosen.

_____

_____

Collective Nouns - 1

1. Below are words that name a collection of animals or things. Use your dictionary to find out what animals or things are in the collection.

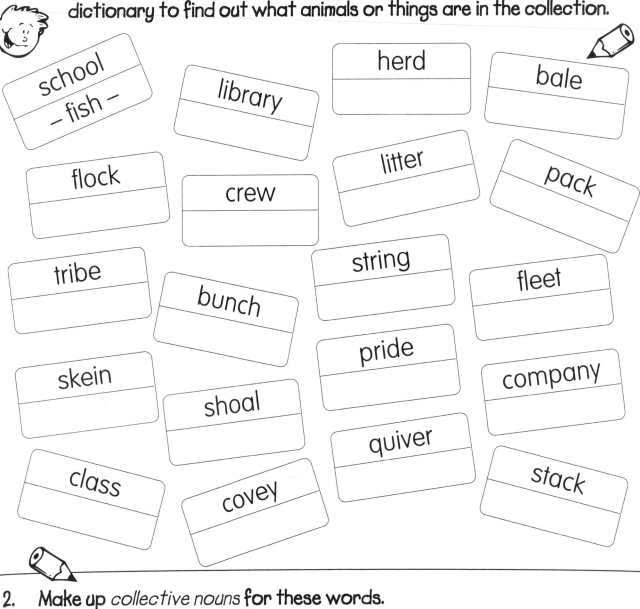

school
– fish –

library

herd

bale

flock

crew

litter

pack

tribe

bunch

string

fleet

skein

shoal

pride

company

class

covey

quiver

stack

2. **Make up** *collective nouns* **for these words.**

(a) pencils _____

(b) leaves _____

(c) files _____

(d) bricks _____

(e) doors _____

(f) staples _____

1. Listed below are *collective nouns*. The animals or things in the collection are hidden in the word search.

Collective Nouns - 2

N	L	W	K	S	L	U	H	O
E	F	O	W	M	I	R	Q	T
X	Y	L	Y	B	O	O	K	S
O	A	V	B	S	N	T	S	B
C	R	E	E	G	S	S	T	I
H	N	S	E	E	R	T	N	R
S	H	D	S	E	D	A	A	D
I	T	V	R	S	N	R	L	S
F	L	O	W	E	R	S	P	H
M	D	R	A	W	E	R	S	L

(a) drove _____

(b) grove _____

(c) flock _____

(d) chest _____

(e) clump _____

(f) library _____

(g) pack _____

(h) school _____

(i) pride _____

(j) galaxy _____

(k) skein _____   (l) swarm _____

(m) bouquet _____   (n) gaggle _____

- -

2. Match these *collective nouns* to their collections.

coven •   • bells

carillon •   • musicians

orchard •   • witches

orchestra •   • fruit trees

1. Use your dictionary to help find the meaning of these *abbreviations*.

(a) G.P.O. _____

(b) Assn. _____

(c) Dr. _____

(d) p.m. _____

(e) Thurs. _____

Abbreviations

2. Match each *abbreviation* to its meaning.

(a) a.m. •   • compact disc

(b) ID •   • cash on delivery

(c) CD •   • before Christ

(d) B.C. •   • ante meridiem
                      (morning)

(e) C.O.D. •   • identification

3. Write *abbreviations* for these words.

(a) anonymous _____

(b) accommodation _____

(c) longitude _____

(d) minimum _____

(e) please turn over _____

1. Name a fruit or vegetable next to each letter of the alphabet.

M	_____	R	_____
A	_____	E	_____
Z	_____	G	_____
O	_____	S	_____
P	_____	W	_____
B	_____	T	_____
L	_____	C	_____

2. Write the fruits and vegetables from above into *alphabetical order*.

_____

_____

_____

_____

_____

_____

3. Unjumble these fruits and put them in *alphabetical order*.
   sgarone, iriikwfut, nrtencaies, eadts

_____

Alphabetical Order - 2

1. List the words below in *alphabetical order*. The words are in pairs, with the first two letters of each pair the same.

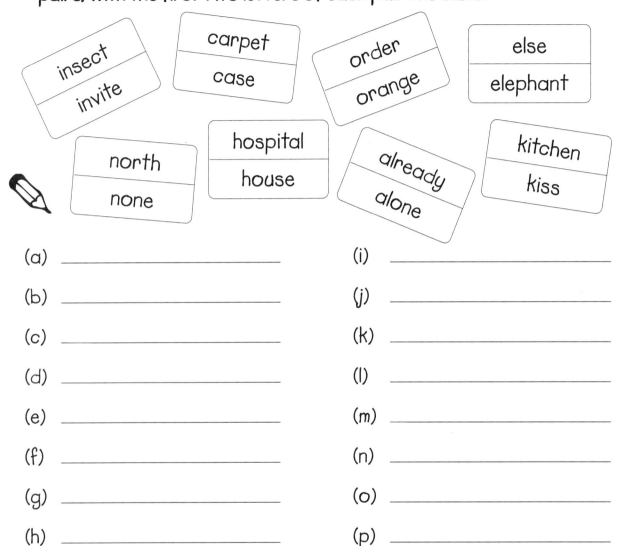

insect / invite

carpet / case

order / orange

else / elephant

north / none

hospital / house

already / alone

kitchen / kiss

(a) _____   (i) _____

(b) _____   (j) _____

(c) _____   (k) _____

(d) _____   (l) _____

(e) _____   (m) _____

(f) _____   (n) _____

(g) _____   (o) _____

(h) _____   (p) _____

2. Find the 'witch' words in the word circle. Write them in *alphabetical order*.

MAGICOVENEWTASTEVILIZADREAM

_____

_____

_____

_____

_____

_____

1. Time how long it takes you to list these words in *alphabetical order.*

worm mountain station fork hundred grate
hunter form mouse grape stamp world
fort grain stand word mouth hungry

(a) _____

(b) _____

(c) _____

(d) _____

(e) _____

(f) _____

(g) _____

(h) _____

(i) _____

(j) _____

(k) _____

(l) _____

(m) _____

(n) _____

(o) _____

(p) _____

(q) _____

(r) _____

Time: _____

2. How many pairs of words can you find
that begin with the same first four letters?
For example, store and storm.

_____

_____

_____

1. **Put these 's' words in** *alphabetical order.*

swam, salt, silver, spring, smell, swim, sugar, snake, shirt, spend, small, splash, secret, skirt

_____   _____

_____   _____

_____   _____

_____   _____

_____   _____

2. **Find three words that begin with each letter. Write them in** *alphabetical order.*

m
_____
_____
_____

d
_____
_____
_____

t
_____
_____
_____

3. **Unjumble the number words and number them in** *alphabetical order.*

otw   _____   ☐

ruof   _____   ☐

teghi   _____   ☐

ether   _____   ☐

xis   _____   ☐

vife   _____   ☐

eon   _____   ☐

neves   _____   ☐

4. **Draw the seasons of the year in** *alphabetical order* **on the back of this page.**

Spring
Summer
Autumn
Winter

Occupations

1. **Complete the word puzzle to find the mystery** *occupation.*

1. A person who helps to keep your teeth in good condition.

2. Someone who designs, builds and uses machines.

3. A person who gives legal advice.

4. A person who studies the composition and reactions of substances.

5. Someone who is trained to fix cars.

```
1 ☐☐☐☐☐☐☐☐☐
2 ☐☐☐☐☐☐
     3 ☐☐☐☐☐☐☐☐
        4 ☐☐☐☐☐☐☐☐☐
     5 ☐☐☐☐☐☐☐
  6 ☐☐☐☐☐☐☐☐
     7 ☐☐☐☐☐☐☐
```

6. A person who installs pipes and fixtures involved with water.

7. Someone who sells flowers.

The mystery occupation is a _____.

---

2. **Match these people to their** *occupations.*

photographer •   • one who writes and presents news articles

zookeeper •   • one who takes photos

police officer •   • one who looks after animals

journalist •   • one who cooks

chef •   • one who prevents crime

1. The young of animals have special names; for example, a baby swan is called a cygnet. Use your dictionary to find the adult or young names for the following animals. Draw a pair in the space provided.

YOUNG	ADULT
cub	
	goat
	eagle
lamb	
fawn	

YOUNG	ADULT
gosling	
whelp	
	cow
	whale
nestling	

2. Unjumble the young and match them to their parents.

lpatdoe •　　　• cat

facl •　　　• dog

ntikte •　　　• frog

ppypu •　　　• hippopotamus

1. **Sort these words into their correct groups.**

badger	acorn	thyme	bamboo
doublet	ark	collie	sloth
kayak	willow	bandolier	trawler
toga	sarong	llama	acacia
beret	elk	sloop	sampan

Which Group?

Animal Words	Ship Words	Clothes Words	Plant Words

2. **Find the words above in the word search. Color the animal words blue, the ship words red, the clothes words yellow and the plant words green.**

L	I	N	O	P	R	E	I	L	O	D	N	A	B
G	N	O	R	A	S	E	I	L	L	O	C	G	A
C	A	M	B	C	L	W	K	E	K	U	A	O	D
N	P	P	E	A	O	O	B	M	A	B	M	T	G
R	M	O	R	C	T	L	H	Y	Y	L	A	C	E
O	A	O	E	I	H	L	T	H	A	E	L	K	R
C	S	L	T	A	L	I	E	T	K	T	L	R	A
A	L	S	T	R	A	W	L	E	R	C	O	A	S

Masculine and Feminine

Find the masculine or feminine for these words. Then complete the word search.

Masculine	Feminine
father	
	queen
	daughter
lion	
buck	
cob	
	ewe
	sow
	mare
	hen
wizard	
gander	
bull	
	tigress
	peahen
merman	

N	N	A	M	R	E	M
O	R	C	Q	H	T	P
I	A	O	U	E	I	E
L	O	W	N	N	G	N
K	B	R	O	M	R	R
I	D	E	I	D	E	E
N	O	D	L	A	S	T
G	E	N	L	U	S	S
O	S	A	A	G	L	O
O	O	G	T	H	I	O
S	W	B	S	T	O	R
E	Q	U	E	E	N	E
M	W	C	W	R	E	H
A	G	K	I	E	S	T
R	A	M	T	G	S	A
E	W	E	C	I	O	F
C	O	B	H	T	N	B
W	I	Z	A	R	D	U
N	E	H	A	E	P	L
M	O	T	H	E	R	L
P	E	A	C	O	C	K
D	I	A	M	R	E	M

1. Use the clues to find the placenames from around the world. You will need an atlas.

Across
1. Paris is the capital of ...
3. Beijing is the capital of ...
6. The capital of the USA is ...
8. The capital of Italy is ...
10. Tokyo is the capital of ...
14. Lima is the capital of ...
15. The capital of the United Kingdom is ...
16. Helsinki is the capital of ...
17. Brasilia is the capital of ...

Down
2. Cairo is the capital of ...
3. Santiago is the capital of...
4. Canberra is the capital of ...
5. Madrid is the capital of ...
6. The capital of New Zealand is ...
7. The capital of Canada is ...
9. Mexico City is the capital of ...
11. The capital of Greece is ...
12. The capital of India is ...
13. The capital of the Republic of Ireland is ...

Adjectives

adjectives are words which describe a noun. They give the reader more information. For example, the **big, brown** dog ate the **fat, juicy** steak quickly.

1. List five *adjectives* to describe your shoe.

   (a) _____

   (b) _____

   (c) _____

   (d) _____

   (e) _____

2. How many *adjectives* can you find in this word circle?

   shardrabraveighthilariousweterrificolorfulu

3. Improve these sentences by including *adjectives* when you rewrite them.

   (a) The girl wore a dress.

   _____

   (b) A spider scared the boy.

   _____

   (c) The bear chased the fox.

   _____

 4. Write five sentences, using adjectives, to describe your favorite possession on the back of this page.

> **Verbs** are action words. For example, walk or run.
> **adverbs** add descriptions to verbs. These tell the reader
> how, where and when it is done. For example, walk slowly
> or run quickly.

Verbs and Adverbs

1. Circle the *verbs* red and *adverbs* blue in these sentences.

    (a) The red train chugged slowly up the steep hill.

    (b) Tracey ran swiftly through the park to collect her sister before it rained heavily.

    (c) Michael walked slowly and lazily to school because he had a science test.

2. Write two *adverbs* for each verb.

    (a) hop _____

    (b) skip _____

    (c) laugh _____

    (d) clap _____

    (e) climb _____

3. Find two synonyms for these adverbs.

    (a) quickly _____ _____

    _____

    (b) slowly _____

    _____

    (c) happily _____

    _____

ANAGRAMS

> An **anagram** is a word formed by rearranging the letters in another word. For example, ate becomes tea or eat.

1. Use these words to find an *anagram* to match the meaning.

Word	Anagram	Meaning
north		a sharp-pointed prickle on the stem of a plant
rats		a heavenly body seen at night
wasp		the feet of an animal with claws or nails
mate		used to being handled by humans
hint		slim or lean

2. Match these words to their *anagram*.

reaps	•	• nails
tools	•	• throw
read	•	• spear
worth	•	• rope
snail	•	• race
pore	•	• stool
acre	•	• dear

3. Can you think of an *anagram* of assume?

_____

4. Think of five more *anagrams*. Share them with your friends.

_____

_____

Compound Words

1. **Match the words in column one with words in column two to make** *compound words.*

Column 1	Column 2	Compound Words
other	string	
butter	print	
shoe	mate	
sea	wise	
ship	fly	
finger	horse	

2. **Add a word to each of these to make a** *compound word.*

   (a) over _____

   (b) _____ fall

   (c) _____ paper

   (d) lady _____

   (e) foot _____

   (f) _____ fire

3. **Find the** *compound words* **in the word search.**

N	E	V	E	R	T	H	E	L	E	S	S
O	Z	P	I	H	S	D	N	E	I	R	F
B	P	S	C	A	M	P	F	I	R	E	R
O	V	E	R	D	U	E	S	A	I	R	T
D	Q	T	E	C	A	L	P	E	R	I	F
Y	M	Y	S	E	L	F	C	U	O	L	A
E	G	N	O	L	E	M	R	E	T	A	W

1. Research to find *new* and interesting *words* related to each of these topics.

BIRDS

BUILDINGS

BOATS

SPORTS

2. Choose a topic that interests you and write five new and interesting words related to it.

1. The words below have something to do with sports, clothes, animals and tools/equipment.

Find out what these words mean and sort them into the correct category.

lens, mallet, chinchilla, bellows, snorkel, sari, athletics, partridge, hurdle, pulley, yak, vice, salamander, ski, elk, poncho, moccasin, archery, smock, sarong

Sports	Clothes	Animals	Tools/Equipment

2. Find five new and interesting words to do with plants.

Word Fun

a **palindrome** is a word or series of words that read the same forwards and backwards. For example, sees.

1. Use the clues to solve the palindromes.

   (a) Babies need this to keep their clothes clean while eating.

   _____

   (b) Another way of saying midday.

   _____

   (c) A small child.

   _____

   (d) The past tense of 'do'.

   _____

   (e) A type of boat.

   _____

   PUP!

a **magic square** is like a crossword puzzle but the answers are the same across and down. For example:

```
B I R D
I
R
D
```

2. Can you solve these word squares?

1. Opposite of give.
2. This chemical can eat away metal.
3. A male ruler.
4. You must be careful of the sharp _____ of a knife.

¹T	²	³	⁴
²			
³		*n*	
⁴			

1	2	3	4
2	**D**		
3			
4			**E**

1. The opposite to tame.
2. A thought or a picture in your mind.
3. The opposite to right.
4. A type of fruit.

1.   Find fifteen pieces of sporting equipment in the word search.

S	U	R	F	B	O	A	R	D	S	M
C	L	U	B	A	G	L	O	V	E	R
T	B	S	E	L	G	G	O	G	P	O
T	E	H	E	L	M	E	T	F	O	F
I	E	L	T	S	I	H	W	I	R	I
M	R	A	C	Q	U	E	T	N	L	N
S	K	A	T	E	B	O	A	R	D	U
E	E	L	C	Y	C	I	B	N	E	T

1. _____

2. _____

3. _____

4. _____

5. _____

6. _____

7. _____   8. _____   9. _____

10. _____   11. _____   12. _____

13. _____   14. _____   15. _____

2.   Guess the sport by the shape of each word.
     football, hockey, swimming, cricket, netball, basketball

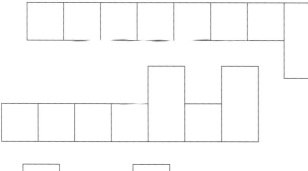

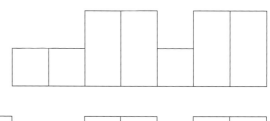

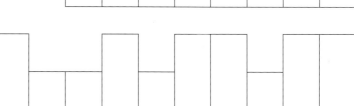

Page 5
1. disappoint, disarm, disagree, disable, disappear, disapprove
   bikini, binoculars, bicentenary, bisect, bicycle, biannual
   unable, uncouth, unpaid, uncover, uneven, unknown
2. Answers may vary

Page 6
1.

Prefix	Meaning	Example
re	again/repetition	answers
sub	below/under	may
mis	wrong/mistaken	vary

2. Answers may vary
3. anti → against, bi → two, auto → self, dis → apart from, not, post → after, pre → before, tri → three, un → not
4. Answers may vary

Page 7
1. repay, rearrange, redo, reprint, rewrite, rewind
2. Teacher check
3. False, true, false, false
4. Teacher check

Page 8
1. (a) painful (b) beautiful (c) frightful (d) useful (e) tasteful
   Sentences may vary
2. Answers may vary

Page 9
1.

Word	Word with suffix	Meaning
Taiwan	Taiwanese	one from Taiwan
chemistry	chemist	one who works in chemistry
geology	geologist	one who works in geology
Japan	Japanese	one from Japan
parent	parenthood	state of being a parent
father	fatherhood	state of being a father
violin	violinist	one who plays the violin
mother	motherhood	state of being a mother
China	Chinese	one from China
guitar	guitarist	one who plays the guitar

2. Answers may vary

Page 10
1. Down: 1. fearless 3. helpless 4. tasteless 5. homeless 7. senseless
   Across: 2. useless 6. careless 8. endless 9. hopeless 10. restless
2. (a) tasteless (b) careless (c) endless (d) homeless

Page 11
1. teaspoonful, mouthful, painful, cupful
2. Teacher check
3. farmer, painter, gardener, baker

Page 12
1. (a) everybody (b) fall (c) remember (d) present (e) midday (f) stale (g) friend (h) apart (i) depart (j) export (k) useless (l) cowardly (m) disobey (n) smooth (o) exit
2. (a) irregular (b) insincere (c) often (d) disrespect

Page 13
1.

	Word	Antonym
rrofwad	forward	backward
tiwner	Winter	Summer
deda	dead	alive
epon	open	shut
nmcnuomo	uncommon	common
olcse	close	open
olw	low	high
ncninoet	innocent	guilty
yanuhpp	unhappy	happy
crocinret	incorrect	correct

2. hate → have → hive → live → love
   wild → wile → tile → time → tame
   fall → fill → file → rile → rise

Page 14
1. last/first, poor/rich, old/young, girl/boy, hot/cold, weak/strong, wet/dry, up/down, on/off, in/out, top/bottom, shallow/deep, day/night, large/small, inside/outside, fast/slow, under/over, wide/narrow, above/below, cry/laugh, high/low
2. Teacher check

Page 15
1. Across: 4. attractive 6. error 7. select 8. mad 9. cheerful 10. journey 12. motor 13. gentle 14. complete
   Down: 1. easy 2. breeze 3. peculiar 5. wood 8. many 9. commence 11. nought
2. Answers may vary

Page 16
1. Answers may vary   2. Answers may vary
3. Answers may vary

Page 17
1. Teacher check
2. close/shut, chair/seat, go/leave, grin/smile, unkind/mean, yell/shout, sleepy/tired, leap/jump
3. (a) pretty (b) easy (c) skinny (d) near (e) almost (f) sea

Page 18
1. (a) flour (b) for/fore (c) bore (d) sail
2. (a) see, tail (b) whole, fair (c) blew, rain, through
3. (a) cue - a long stick used to hit a ball in billiards.
   (b) queue - a single line of people, cars, animals, etc., waiting in turn for something.
   (c) quay - a wharf where ships and ferries load or unload passengers or cargo.
   (d) key - a small specially-shaped piece of metal that can open a lock.

Page 19
1. Across: 2. where 5. hear 6. witch 8. pear 10. eye 11. steel 12. cheap 15. ate 16. write
   Down: 1. wore 2. weigh 3. bale 4. there 7. cent 8. poll 9. new 11. sea 13. plain 14. male
2. Teacher check   3. Answers may vary

Page 20
1. Teacher check
2. Teacher check
3. bill, stick, cricket - Teacher check

Page 21
1. (a) they'll (b) haven't (c) there's (d) we're (e) you've (f) I'm (g) let's (h) I'd
2. (a) haven't, hasn't (b) shouldn't, (c) should've, I'll
3. (a) that's (b) could've (c) they'd (d) where's

Page 22

1. do not/don't, that is/that's, it is/it's, is not/isn't, we have/we've, they have/they've, did not/didn't, you have/you've, she is/she's, what is/what's, were not/weren't, I have/I've
2. let's, won't, I'm
3. we've, they've, you've, I've
   isn't, don't, didn't, weren't
   what's, she's, it's, that's
4. What's, She's, you've, weren't

Page 23

1. men, children, feet, women
2. (a) echoes (b) bunches (c) dresses (d) potatoes (e) boxes (f) glasses (g) brushes (h) lunches
3. 1. chimneys 2. holidays 3. lollies 4. enemies 5. daisies 6. flies

Page 24

1. (a) knife (b) calves (c) leaves (d) loaf
2. fingers, shelves, tomatoes, benches, keys, fairies, wishes, kisses, lives, days, monkeys, butterflies, foxes, wolves, cargoes, sheep

Page 25

1.

Word	Meaning
astro	star
derm	skin
geo	earth
phon	sound
photo	light
aqua	water
circum	around
forma	shape
scribe	write
bene	well

2. Answers may vary

Page 26

1. school = fish, library = books, herd = cows/cattle etc. bale = wool/hay, flock = sheep/birds, litter = pups/kittens, crew = sailors, tribe = people, bunch = flowers/grapes, string = pearls, fleet = ships, pack = cards/wolves, skein = wool, shoal = fish, pride = lions, company = soldiers, class = students, stack = papers/bricks/hay, covey = partridges, quiver = arrows
2. Answers may vary.

Page 27

1. (a) oxen (b) trees (c) birds (d) drawers (e) trees (f) books (g) cards/wolves (h) fish (i) lions (j) stars (k) wool (l) bees (m) flowers (n) geese
2. coven → witches, carillon → bells, orchestra → musicians, orchard → fruit trees

Page 28

1. (a) General Post Office (b) Association (c) Doctor (d) post meridiem (e) Thursday
2. (a) a.m. - ante meridiem (b) ID - identification (c) CD - compact disc (d) B.C. - before Christ (e) C.O.D. - cash on delivery
3. (a) anon. (b) accom. (c) long. (d) min. (e) p.t.o.

Page 29

1. Answers may vary
2. A, B, C, E, G, L, M, O, P, R, S, T, W, Z
3. dates, kiwifruit, nectarines, oranges

Page 30

1. (a) alone (b) already (c) carpet (d) case (e) elephant (f) else (g) hospital (h) house (i) insect (j) invite (k) kiss (l) kitchen (m) none (n) north (o) orange (p) order
2. coven, dream, evil, lizard, magic, newt, taste

Page 31

1. (a) fork (b) form (c) fort (d) grain (e) grape (f) grate (g) hundred (h) hungry (i) hunter (j) mountain (k) mouse (l) mouth (m) stamp (n) stand (o) station (p) word (q) world (r) worm
2. Answers may vary

Page 32

1. salt, secret, shirt, silver, skirt, small, smell, snake, spend, splash
2. Answers may vary
3. two 8, four 3, eight 1, three 7, six 6, five 2, one 4, seven 5
4. Answers may vary

Page 33

1. 1. dentist 2. engineer 3. lawyer 4. chemist 5. mechanic 6. plumber 7. florist - Mystery occupation is a teacher
2. photographer → one who takes photos, chef → one who cooks, zookeeper → one who looks after animals, police officer → one who prevents crime, journalist → one who writes and presents news articles

Page 34

1. cub/bear, fox, lion; kid/goat; eaglet/eagle; lamb/sheep; fawn/deer; gosling/goose; whelp/dog, wolf, bear, lion, tiger, seal; calf/cow; calf/whale; nestling/bird
2. tadpole → frog, calf → hippopotamus, kitten → cat, puppy → dog

Page 35

1.

Animal Words	Ship Words	Clothes Words	Plant Words
badger	ark	doublet	acorn
collie	kayak	bandolier	thyme
sloth	trawler	toga	bamboo
llama	sampan	sarong	willow
elk	sloop	beret	acacia

2. Teacher check

Page 36

father/mother, king/queen, son/daughter, lion/lioness, buck/doe, cob/pen, ram/ewe, boar/sow, stallion/mare, rooster/hen, wizard/witch, gander/goose, bull/cow, tiger/tigress, peacock/peahen, merman/mermaid

Page 37

1. Across: 1. France 3. China 6. Washington 8. Rome 10. Japan 14. Peru 15. London 16. Finland 17. Brazil
   Down: 2. Egypt 3. Chile 4. Australia 5. Spain 6. Wellington 7. Ottawa 9. Mexico 11. Athens 12. New Delhi 13. Dublin

Page 38

1. Answers may vary
2. drab, brave, eighth, hilarious, sweet, terrific, colourful, lush, hard
3. Answers may vary
4. Answers may vary

Page 39

1. (a) verb - chugged — adverb - slowly
   (b) verbs - ran, collect, rained — adverbs - swiftly, heavily
   (c) verbs - walked, had — adverbs - slowly, lazily
2. Answers may vary
3. Answers may vary

Page 40

1. thorn, star, paws, tame, thin
2. reaps - spear, tools - stool, read - dear, worth - throw, snail - nails, pore - rope, acre - race
3. assume - amuses
4. Answers may vary

Page 41

1. otherwise, butterfly, shoestring, seahorse, shipmate, fingerprint
2. Answers may vary
3. nevertheless, friendship, campfire, overdue, fireplace, myself, watermelon, nobody

Page 42

1. Answers may vary
2. Answers may vary

Page 43

1.

Sports	Clothes	Animals	Tools/Equipment
snorkel	sari	chinchilla	lens
athletics	smock	partridge	mallet
hurdle	moccasin	yak	bellows
ski	poncho	salamander	vice
archery	sarong	elk	pulley

2. Answers may vary

Page 44

1. (a) bib (b) noon (c) tot (d) did (e) kayak
2.

T	A	K	E
A	C	I	D
K	I	N	G
E	D	G	E

W	I	L	D
I	D	E	A
L	E	F	T
D	A	T	E

Page 45

1. surfboard, glove, skateboard, net, balls, bicycle, goggles, club, bag, bat, rope, skate, tee, oar, helmet
2. Teacher check